Something to Know

REV. C. C. HENRY, SR.

NEWMAN SPRINGS PUBLISHING
320 Broad Street
Red Bank, NJ 07701

First originally published by Newman Springs Publishing 2022

ISBN 978-1-68498-965-2 (Paperback)
ISBN 978-1-68498-966-9 (Digital)

Printed in the United States of America

Man Losing the Image of God

From the book of Genesis chapter 1, in the beginning, God created the heaven and earth (the earth is the Lord and the fullness thereof; the world and, they, that dwell therein [Psalm 24:1]). The earth and everything in it are God's creations, so no man can be credited for it.

In the beginning, the beginning of the creation, not the beginning of God existent, for God was before the creation and is self-existing, no explanation needed.

Now that we have established and accepted that God is the creator of all things in heaven and earth, for the heavens declare the glory of God, and the firmament showeth his handy work (Psalm 19:1), all things were created by the power of God's word (let there be, and there it was).

The Plan for Man

When it comes to the creation of man, it becomes personal; let us make man, and man has become his personal creation, hands-on, which created a relationship and fellowship between God and man.

In Genesis 1:26, "And God said, let us make man in our own Image, after our likeness." The plurality of us and our can only be referred to the Father, Son, and Spirit (John1:1,2).

So God created man in his own Image. (Genesis 1:27)

The image of God is the characteristics of God: the spiritual man, the righteous man, and the holy man is the image of God, created he-him (male and female) and created he-them.

The species is man, and the gender is male and female (their task was to multiply and replenish the earth). The male carries the seeds, while the female delivers the seeds. Every man (male and female) are in the population of man from creations.

The Lord God said, "Let us make man in our own image and likeness." What is God's image and likeness?

I believe the image of God is Spirit, holiness, and righteousness (God is a Spirit, and they that worship him must worship him in spirit and truth [John 4:24]). Holiness without which no man shall see God (Hebrews 12:14b). "Righteousness, art thou, O Lord" (Psalms 119:137a).

And His likeness is His beauty, will, love, the ability to be creative, etc. Every man (male or female) God created is beautiful; there are no flaws in them; before Adam sinned, Adam contaminated them.

Every man (male or female) was given a will of their own, which gave them a right to make their own choices between good and evil. Every man (male or female) is capable of love, which is of a godly nature to love someone or something.

Every man (male or female) was given a purpose and was creative in some sort of way.

Male and Female

God has created all the creatures of the earth, the fowls of the air, and the fishes of the sea in pairs, male and female, for the multiplication of each species on earth, air, and sea.

The Lord God gave man the same task, so He made them male and female for the multiplication of the human race. It cannot be any other way.

Two males cannot have babies, neither can two females have babies. It takes a male and a female to have babies for the population of the human race. It is so ordained by God Himself.

> And God blessed them, and God said unto them,
> be fruitful and multiply and replenish the earth.
> (Genesis 1:28)

And God said unto them, them in plural, they need each other for the task.

And the Lord God formed man of the dust of the ground (gives man a connection with the earth) and breathed into his nostril the breath of life, and man became a living soul, a connection with God with a body, soul, and spirit. The creation of man from the earth gives man the attachment and authority over all the creation, which God entrusted unto him (Genesis 2:7).

God provides man with home and provisions.

> And the Lord God planted a garden eastward in
> Eden (First given location), and there he put the
> man whom he had formed. (Genesis 2:8)

This garden was man's home, and he was supposed to eat, sleep, and live without the rest of the animals, even though he had access to all the animals.

> And out of the ground made the Lord God to
> grow every tree that is pleasant to the sight and
> good for food; the tree of life also in the mist of
> the garden, and the tree of knowledge of good
> and evil. (Genesis 2:9)

Note here that every tree that was planted in the garden, including the tree of life, is pleasant to the sight and good for food. But the tree of knowledge of good and evil, which was in the garden, was the only tree in the garden that was off-limits.

Man could have eaten of the tree of life, which was the fruit of the Spirit, and the fruit of the Spirit consists of these fruits: love, joy, peace, long-suffering, gentleness, goodness, faith, meekness, and temperance.

The tree of good and evil is forbidden because its main ingredients were full of wickedness and produced fleshly desires, such as adultery, fornication, uncleanness, hatred, lasciviousness, idolatry, witchcraft, variance, emulations, wrath, strife, seditions, heresies, envying, and reveling, which are all poisonous and deadly.

Man's First Instruction

> And the Lord God took the man (the male known as Adam) put him into the garden of Eden to dress it and keep it.
>
> And the Lord God commanded the man (the male) saying, "Of every tree of the garden thou mayst freely eat (Adam was free to eat of every tree, including the tree of life);
>
> But of the tree of knowledge of good and evil, thou shall not eat of it (warning before destruction); for in the day that thou eatest thereof thou shalt surely die." (Genesis 2:15–17)

The instruction was not grievous but was precise because if you eat off this tree, you will die. The fruit of the tree of knowledge of good and evil, which some call an apple, is more deadly than any apple. Its fruits are the fruits of sin and death (God's intention here was for the man not to have any knowledge of good and evil but to remain in His image of innocence). Eating from the tree of knowledge of good and evil carries a penalty (death).

The death here is not referring only to the physical death but also to the spiritual death as well, which makes man die in the image of God. Though the fellowship and the relationship between God and man was broken, man could regain the fellowship and relationship through prayer and sacrifice to God on his own but not in his image. Only through the ultimate sacrifice of Jesus Christ, His only begotten Son, the image of God can be restored to man, and man must accept the sacrifice that Jesus Christ made on the cross.

The Female

Genesis 2:18 introduces the plan for the female and her purpose:

> And the Lord God said, "It is not good that the man should be alone; I will make him a helper meet for him."

"A helper meet for him" means the female, not only for companionship and domestic purposes, helps multiply and replenish the earth.

Man was given the authority to name all of God's creations (Genesis 2:19, 20)

> And the Lord God caused a deep sleep to fall upon Adam and he slept; and he took one of his ribs, and closed up the flesh instead thereof (it was the first surgery performed on man by God);
> And the rib, which the Lord God had taken from man (male) made He a woman (female, a man with a womb) and brought her to Adam.
> And Adam said, "This is now bone of my bones, and flesh of my flesh (a relationship), she shall be called Woman because she was taken out of man." (Genesis 2:21–23)

Note here is that was the only time that a man gives birth, for the woman was taken out of him by operation of his Creator; He is the potter, and we are the clay.

The woman was taken out of the man, which started the chain connection of all human beings, regardless of race, color, or creed; we are all connected to Adam, and Adam is connected to the earth.

The First Marriage and Vow

Therefore shall a man leave his father and mother, and shall cleave unto his wife; and they shall be one flesh.

And they were both naked, the man and his wife, and were not ashamed. (Genesis 2:24–25)

There is no room for two of the same gender. Everything is going according to God's plan, and man has been created, given a home, and given authority over all the creatures on earth, even if you name them. Adam was given instructions on how to live a long and prosperous life, given a wife, and have a relationship and fellowship with the Lord God Himself and are still in the image of God.

The Fall of Man and Losing the Image of God

Now the serpent was more subtle (crafty) than any beast of the field which the Lord God had made. And he said unto the woman, "Yea, hath God said, 'Ye shall not eat of *every* tree of the garden'?" (Genesis 3:1)

I believe the temptation of the woman (Eve) not yet named was not in the garden of Eden, their home, for Adam would have known about it, so she was away from her home and the security of Adam. Note:

1. She should have been by her husband's side.
2. She shouldn't be having any conversation with any of the beasts of the field.
3. The formation of the serpent's question to get information should have caught her attention: "God said ye shall not eat **of every** tree in the garden?" She should have known that was a lie and walked away.

4. It is obvious that the serpent didn't know which tree either or its location God had warned them about. He was seeking information.

5. She gave the information the serpent was seeking for.

> And the woman said unto the serpent, "We may eat of the fruit of the trees of the garden,
>
> but of the fruit of the tree which is in the mist of the garden (location given), God hath said, 'Ye shall not eat of it, neither shall ye touch it, lest ye die.'" (Genesis 3:2)

> And the Lord God commanded the man, saying, "Of every tree of the garden thou mayest freely eat;
>
> but of the tree of knowledge of good and evil, thou shalt not eat of it: for the day that thou eatest thereof thou shalt surely die."
>
> And the Lord God said, "It is not good that the man should be alone; I will make him a helper meet for him." (Genesis 2:16–18)

The woman here added another condition to the danger of the tree, even if you only touch it, you'll die. The serpent responded to her with a lie that sounded like the truth:

> And the serpent said unto her, "Ye shall not surely die (the art of deception were instigated by the serpent);
>
> For God doth know that in that day ye eat thereof, then your eyes shall be opened, and ye shall be as gods, knowing good and evil." (Genesis 3:4–5)

There were some truths in that saying that their eyes would be open to know good and evil, but the lie was that they wouldn't die, and they would become a god.

The woman knew the truth but listened to the lies.

> She took of the fruit thereof and did eat, and gave
> also unto her husband with her, and he did eat.

The serpent did not deceive the man, but the woman and the man had the option here not to partake of eating the fruit the woman gave to him, and he had firsthand information about eating the fruit, and the result of eating that fruit is forbidden. God Himself had instructed him. The entire world population was in Adam and depended on Adam's decision. That's why we inherited Adam's sin. Every conception of a child, whether a day or a month old, is in the plan of God and was in Adam and has a right to live.

The question asked here is, was Adam afraid of losing the only woman he knows, knowing what it was to be without a companion? Was it because she was bone of his bones and flesh of his flesh? Or his love for her that he was willing to die with her and plunge all of mankind unto death? Just as God so loved the world, He gave His only begotten Son as a living sacrifice to save the world and give everlasting life to all that believed in Him (John 3:16).

Their Eyes Were Opened

> And the eyes of them both were opened, and they
> knew that they were naked. (Genesis 3:7)

Their clothing of innocence was removed, and for the first time, they saw themselves naked and were ashamed of what they saw. And they sewed fig leaves together and made themselves aprons. Eating the fruit of good and evil had revealed to them something they were not aware of and tried to cover up. Even in today's world, we will try to do anything to cover up our sins.

Man Lost the Image and Fellowship with God

> And they heard the voice of the Lord God walk-
> ing in the garden in the cool of the day; and
> Adam and his wife hid themselves from the pres-
> ence of the Lord God amongst the trees of the
> garden. (Genesis 3:8)

Adam and his wife (she wasn't named Eve yet) knew what they had done and went and hid; they heard His voice as they were accustomed to, but it was different, not joyful but angry. They have broken the trust by being disobedient; the fellowship they had with the Lord God before they ate the fruit of the tree of good and evil was over, and they couldn't face the Lord God anymore because they were ashamed, so they went and hid (sometimes if it were possible, we feel like hiding ourselves for the things we have done, but you can't hide from God).

> And the Lord God called unto Adam, and said
> unto him, "Where art thou?" (Genesis 3:9)

I believed God knew where Adam and his wife was, but Adam and his wife heard His voice but didn't know where he was.

> And he said, "I heard thy voice in the garden,
> and I was afraid, because I was naked; and I hid
> myself." (Genesis 3:10)

Adam had just confessed to his predicament, knowing what he had done, and he could not face his master in the state he was, so he could hear His voice, but he couldn't see His face; Adam had not just lost fellowship with God but also the image of God. No man born of a woman after Adam's sin was born in the image of God ever since Adam's sin but in the image of Adam.

> And Adam lived an hundred and thirty years, and
> begat a son in his own likeness, after his image;
> and called his name Seth. (Genesis 5:3)

Only Jesus Christ, born of a woman, was born in the image of God through virgin birth.

> Behold, a virgin shall be with child, and shall
> bring forth a son, and they shall call his name
> Emmanuel (which interpreted is, "God with
> us"). (Matthew 1:23)

Man has lost the image of God, and the relationship and fellowship was broken. Because of sin, there is no intimacy between God and man. God loves us and wants to restore us in His Image but only through His Son, Christ Jesus, "Who is the image of the invisible God, the first born of every creature" (Colossians 1:15)

Naked before God

> And he said, "Who told thee that thou wast
> naked? Hast thou eaten of the tree, whereof I
> commanded thee that thou shouldest not eat?"
> (Genesis 3:11)

Adam did not answer yes or no, but the *man* went directly to the blame game and tried to wiggle out of his responsibility. It's not my fault. No one had to tell Adam, and they were naked; their eyes were opened, and for the first time, they saw their own nakedness, and they were ashamed of what they saw.

> And the man said, "The woman whom thou gav-
> est to be with me, she gave me of the tree, and I
> did eat." (Genesis 3:12)

There is no evidence here, which was said that the woman forced him or pleaded with him to eat the fruit, but it seems to be voluntary.

> And the Lord God said unto the woman, "What is this that thou hast done?" And the woman said, "The serpent beguiled me, and I did eat." (Genesis 3:13)

They knew that they were guilty even though they tried to blame someone else. We all know that when we have done something wrong, even if we say someone else encourages us to do it, we inherit it from Adam by him eating the tree of knowledge of good and evil.

> The serpent was punished, and his punishment was a curse, to crawl on its belly and dust was its food for the rest of its life.
> From now on you and the woman will be enemies, and her offspring shall crush his head, and he shall bruise his heel. (Genesis 3:14–15)

Verse 15 was of the messianic prophecies; the Messiah was bruised on the cross on Mount Calvary.

> Unto the woman He said, "I will greatly multiply thy sorrow and thy conception; in sorrow thou shall bring forth children; and thy desire shall be to thy husband, and he shall rule over thee." (Genesis 3:16)

It appears here that childbearing should be painless to the woman at the time of conception with some or no discomfort, but now, because she listens to the serpent, childbearing would be painful with suffering, and that was the punishment for the woman.

And unto Adam he said, "Because thou hast hearkened unto the voice of thy wife, and has eaten
of the tree of which I commanded thee, saying,
'Thou shalt eat not of it;' cursed is the ground
for thy sake; in sorrow shalt thou eat of till all the
days of thy life.'" (Genesis 3:17)

Because thou hast hearkened (listened) to the voice of thy wife
(the voice of thy wife, the voice of thy mother, father, brother, friend,
or any voice that encourage you to do whatever you know is wrong;
you and you alone must accept the consequence and not blaming
another for the choices you make in life).

Cursed Is the Ground

Thorns also and thistles shall it bring forth to
thee; and thou shalt eat of the herb of the field.
(Genesis 3:18)

Adam's disobedience did not only affect himself but also all
mankind, creatures of the land, sea, and air, for everything was taken
out of the ground, and Adam has a connection to the ground, for he
was made out of the ground, and everything that created was for the
comfort of man, and so he gave man authority over all creature's and
to name them.

The earth was commanded to bring forth thorns and thistles;
not only did the earth bring forth thorns and thistles and whatever
it desires, such as earthquakes, volcanoes, flies, roaches, mosquitoes,
and anything that will make man uncomfortable for his sin, the
beast of the field, the birds of the air, and the fishes of the sea, but
had turned against man who once has authority over them; man has
become their enemy.

Because of Adam's sin, the air also produces hurricanes, tor-
nadoes, and strong winds; the sea produces tsunami, storms, high
waves, etc.

> And the Lord God said, "Behold, the man is become as one of us, to know good and evil." (Genesis 3:22)

God here acknowledges that man now knows what's good and evil, which makes him responsible for his own actions. I believed it was God's intention for the man to remain in his innocent state and wouldn't have to choose anyway, but the man hearkens to the voice of his wife, and the wife hearkens to the voice of the serpent, and man hid when he heard the voice of the Lord God.

And now, he puts forth his hand and takes also of the tree of life and eats to live forever. Because of the man's ability to choose, if it were possible, that man could get to the tree of life and eat that fruit; man would have lived in that sinful state for the rest of his life and would never die.

Christ Jesus, the only begotten Son of God, who was there in the plan of all creations and also in the plan of redemption of man if man messes up.

The Lord God knew that Adam could sin because of his will and notified him of the danger of eating the tree of good and evil, but God did not prejudge Adam but put all in perspective and preparation for the salvation of man and His most valuable and unique possession on earth; one that He created with His own hand if he sinned.

Christ Jesus, the only begotten Son of God, represented the tree of life, His death on the cross, hanging from a tree, and He could boldly say to the repented thief beside Him today, "Thou shalt be with me in paradise." The garden of Eden, which is paradise, has been regained.

I believe that every born-again believer dies, dying in Christ Jesus, and goes back to the garden of Eden and not to heaven, as some had stated.

While man covered himself with fig leaves to cover his shame, and the fig leaves will rot; God gave them a more appropriate covering, more durable and will last longer than the fig leaves, a covering of skin.

> Therefore, the Lord God sent him forth from the garden of Eden (man's first eviction), to till the ground from whence he was taken. (Genesis 3:23)

Provision was made for him while he was in the garden; now, he must provide for himself and his wife by the sweat on his face is the only way he can eat.

> So he drove out the man; and he placed at the east of the garden of Eden, Cherubims, and a flaming sword which turned every way, to keep the way of the tree of life. (Genesis 3:24)

It appears here that there is only one entrance into the garden where the tree of life is planted, and it is well protected and guarded by the Cherubims with flaming swords so that no man can just walk in and eat the tree of life.

Adam's Sin Produce the Evidence of Good and Evil

> And Adam knew Eve his wife; and she conceived, and bore Cain, and said, "I have gotten a man from the Lord."
> And she again bore his brother Abel (the brothers represents good and evil). (Genesis 4:1–2a)

Cain represents evil, Abel represents good, and the tree of good and evil has been established. And so dwelleth in every man (male and female) good and evil.

May the good part of man overcome the evil part, and God helps us all. Amen.

Adam's sin brings forth death to all, both man and beast. Nothing would have died if it were not for Adam's disobedience.

Adam's sin also brings death to the spiritual man and the physical man.

Jesus Christ's physical death brings life to the spiritual man, and that's why ye must be born again for the spiritual man to be resurrected in you.

Every man, according to God's plan, in the beginning, was created in God's image, but after Adam's sin, no man was born in the image of God, except for Jesus Christ, who was born of a virgin birth.

> "Behold a virgin shall be with child, and shall bring forth a son, and they shall call his name Emmanuel" (which being interpreted is, "God with us"). (Matthew 1:23)

> Then said Mary unto the angel, "How shall this be, seeing I know not a man?" (Luke 1:34)

Mary's pregnancy was not contaminated by a sinful man, but her pregnancy was by the Holy Ghost. In the eyes of God, you are special; you are wonderfully made. If this world were pottery, God is the potter, and you are the clay, whom He formed and fashioned with His own hands and in His own likeness.

In the eyes of God, you are not too small or big, short or tall, skinny or fat, black or white, and red or yellow. You may feel unloved, but God loves you with His love for you through Jesus Christ, His only begotten Son; you try to push Him away, but He won't leave you alone because He loves you just as you are. He loves you.

If this world were a painter's canvas, then God is the only artist that paints such beautiful scenery and a living portrait of you that moves and breathes and has its being. And in the eyes of God, you are one of His precious masterpieces and not just a piece of canvas with a painting but one that is signed, sealed, and framed with the precious blood of His Son, Christ Jesus.

If this world were a botanical garden, God is the biologist; in the eyes of God, you are one of the plants He grafted into the tree of life and are preserved and groomed, which He manicures with His love and life eternal.

If this world were a zoo, then God was the zoologist, a specialist that studies you, your behavior, and your characteristics and divinely applies with kindness and love all your necessary needs.

If this world were a field of jewels, then God is the jeweler, and in His eyes, you are unique and precious. If you are broken, only He can fix you like no other can. He designs and fashions you in beauty and adores you with His grace and places you with His collections of diamonds, rubies, jasper, emeralds, gold, and pearls. To name a few of His treasures, you are most precious to Him.

If this world were a museum, then God is the one that designs such awesome displays of you, not as an artifact that cannot move but as one that is alive in His collections. In the eyes of God, you are one of His most precious in His gallery of exhibits.

If this world were a vineyard, God is the husbandman. In His eyes, you are a branch of His vine, and He expected you to be fruitful, and if you don't, He will prune you, dig around you, and fertilize you so that you can bring forth much fruit. He is just that patient with you.

If the world seemed to be in darkness, and the sun and moon cannot illuminate it, in the eyes of God, you are that light that shines into the darkness that leads those that are in darkness to that great light (Jesus Christ). So let your light shine before men that they may see your good works and glorify your Father in heaven.

God Is Ready to Restore Man Back to His Image

> For God so loved the world, that he gave his only begotten Son, that whosoever believeth in him should not perish, but have everlasting life.
>
> For God sent not his Son into the world to condemn the world; but that the world through him might be saved. (John 3:16–17)

In a world that is full of great buildings, palaces, castles, and cathedrals that are made to accommodate kings and royalties, popes and presidents, there is no building large enough to contain the God of creation, yet there is room in your heart, if you let him in, for He said in Revelation 3:20, "Behold, I stand at the door, and knock, if any man hear my voice, and open the door, I will come in and sup with him, and he with me."

All you have to do right now, wherever you are, is repent of your sins and acknowledge that you are a sinner and in need of a Savior, which is Christ Jesus. Confess and accept Jesus Christ as your Lord, Savior, and Redeemer. Get baptized, and thou shall be saved.

Glory Be to God
Tithing and Offering

Understanding the Concept of Tithe and Offering

Tithing a 10 percent of all one possesses, a requirement for the Jewish nation, as a contribution to the work of the ministries and an inheritance for the tribe of the Levites and priests with a providential clause to take care of the widows, orphans, and strangers. It is not mandatory in the New Testament Church.

I am not trying to confuse or discourage anyone not to give to the church, for the church needs every financial help that can be given to it in this world today.

The Introduction of Tithing or a Tenth

And Melchizedek king of Salem brought forth bread and wine: and he was the priest of the most high God.

And he blessed him, and said, "Blessed be Abram of the most high God, possessor of heaven and earth:

And blessed be the most high God, which hath delivered thine enemies into thy hand." And he gave him tithes of all. (Genesis 14:18–20)

The First Account of Tithe and Voluntary

Abram had just defeated three kings and was on his way back to his home in the land of Mam're, which is in Hebron. When he was met by King Melchizedek, who brought bread and wine for him and his soldiers and in congratulations of their victory, Melchizedek, king and high priest of the most high God in the land of Salem, blessed Abram. In gratitude, Abram presents an offering to Melchizedek.

Abram gave him tithes or a tenth of *all* the spoils he had gotten in victory over the enemies. Dedicated to the most high God, it is fitting that we should express our thankfulness to the most high God by giving some special gift in honor to God. Jesus Christ, our great Melchizedek (Hebrews 7:5–9), is to have homage done Him and to be humbly acknowledged by every one of us as our king and priest; and not only the tithe of all but have must be surrendered and given up to Him.

Tithes or a Tenth with Conditions

And Jacob vowed a vow, saying, "If God will be with me, and will keep me in the way that I go, and will give me bread to eat, and raiment to put on.

So that I come again to my father's house in peace; then shall the Lord be my God:

And this stone, which I have set for a pillar, shall be God's house: and of *all* that thou shalt give me I will surely give the tenth unto thee." (Genesis 28:20–22)

Sometimes we find ourselves in situations whereby we make vows or promises that we only intend to keep if everything goes all right, and sometimes it doesn't.

Jacob vowed a vow, Jacob's modesty and great moderation in his desire to give a tenth of his substance to God. He will cheerfully be content himself with bread to eat and clothes to wear. Jacob's piety and his regard for God, which appears here, were his desires for God to be with him, provides for his food and clothes, and his divine protection to bring him back to his father's house.

The Importance of Tithing

A law concerning tithes, which were paid for the service of God before the law, appears by Abraham (Genesis 14:20), and Jacob promises to God (Genesis 28:22).

> "'And all the tithe of the land, whether of the seed of the land, or of the fruit of the tree, is the Lord's: it is Holy unto the Lord.
>
> And if a man will at all redeem aught of his tithes, he shall add thereto a fifth part thereof.
>
> And concerning the tithe of the herd or of the flock, even of whatsoever passeth under the rod, a tenth shall be holy unto the Lord.
>
> He shall not search whether it be good or bad, neither shall he change it; and if he change it at all, then both it and the change thereof shall be holy; it shall not be redeemed.'" (Leviticus 27:30–33)

It is here appointed that they should pay tithes of all, whether it's from the land or the fruit of the trees or the first fruit of the animals. We are taught here to honor God with our substance, "Honor the Lord with thy substance, and with the first fruits of all thine increase" (Proverbs 3:9–10).

> And if a man will at all redeem (or buy back) ought of his tithes, he shall add therein the fifth (fifth) part thereof. (Leviticus 27:31)

God taught the Israelites that when they made a vow to Him, they must not go back on it, for if they do, there is an increase of a fifth added to whatever they had a vow.

When thou vowest a vow unto God, defer not to pay it, for he hath no pleasure in fools, pay that which thou hast vow.

Better is it that thou shouldest not vow, than to vow and pay not. (Ecclesiastes 5:4–5)

Leviticus 27:30–33 says that a tenth of all that the land produces is to be "Holy to the Lord." The underlying concept is that the tithe is "rent or lease," which Israel owes to God for the use of His land.

The Tithe Becomes an Inheritance for the Tribe of the Levites

And the Lord spoke unto Aaron, "Thou shalt have no inheritance in their land, neither shalt thou have any part among them: I am thy part and thy inheritance among the children of Israel.

And, behold, I have given the children of Levi all the tenth in Israel for an inheritance, for their service, even the service of the tabernacle of the congregation.

Neither must the children of Israel henceforth come nigh themselves the tabernacle of the congregation, lest they bear sin, and die.

But the Levites shall do the service of the tabernacle of the congregation, and they shall bear their iniquity: it shall be a statue forever throughout your generations, that among the children of Israel they shall have no inheritance.

But the Tithes of the children of Israel, which they offer as an heave or waving offering unto the Lord, I have given to the Levites to Inherit: therefore I have said unto them, Among the children of Israel they shall have no inheritance." (Numbers 18:20–24)

All the tithes of the land were given to the Levites that were intended for the Lord, but by God's permission, it was given to them as their only inheritance in the land, and their task was to take care of the services and the tabernacle.

The provision was made both for the Levites and the priests, for they have no inheritance in the land. They must dwell in the city, which allowed them, but no ground for them to occupy.

Numbers 18:20–24 tells us that the tithe was to be used to maintain the Levites, who would receive no tribal land when in Canaan for their inheritance.

When it comes to tithing in the New Testament Church, the most used scripture by our leaders today is Mal.3:8-10, "Will a man rob God?"

The Israelites weren't withholding their tithes and offering, but when they gave, they gave their worst, and God said through Malachi centuries later, calling on His people to obey the law of the tithe.

> "Bring ye *all* the tithes into the storehouse, that there may be meat in mine house, and prove me now herewith," said the Lord of hosts, "If I will not open you the windows of heaven, and pour you out a blessing, that there shall not be room enough to receive it." (Malachi 3:10)

Those who tithed not only kept a divine commandment but also expressed confidence in God's ability to provide for them.

They weren't robbing God not by giving of the tenth but were robbing God by giving of their worst.

The New Testament
Offering or Free-Will Offering

When it comes to the New Testament Church, there is no passage found that imposes tithe as an obligation or mandatory setting of tithing on Christians. Though there is a guiding principle of giving in the church, it should be considered a free-will offering.

The New Testament Church begins its giving with 100 percent of those who give.

> Neither was there any among them that lacked: for as many as were possessors of lands and houses sold them, and brought the prices of the things that were sold,
> And laid them down at the apostles' feet: and distribution was made unto every man according as he had need. (Acts 4:34–35)

I believe every born-again Christians has a desire to give and gives to the best of their ability, but the problem is, some feel guilty because they are not able to give as much as the other person or the required tenth imposed upon them by their leaders, and it makes them feel like they are robbing God because when it comes to giving, all they can hear is, "Will a man rob God?" and not give as God has prospered you, and give it from your heart.

It is encouraged that everyone should give to the house of God, as God has prospered them regularly and cheerfully and not out of necessity and should not be pressured to give but should be taught how to give. The church has a need for money for its operating system in the world and should also have a storehouse for the distributions to the poor, the widows, and orphans. It's a missionary ministry. Giving to the church should be called a free-will offering and not tithing. For there is no set percentage on how much to give, and all should be given from the heart.

Tithing in the Old Testament

Tithing is a commandment. Tithing is a tenth of all: first fruit, first produce, and firstlings of the flocks and herd. It's the reward or inheritance to the Levites for their service in the temple. A tenth of the tenth was given to the priest for their portion of their inheritance.

A special tenth was to be collected every third year for the poor and the needy. Tithing is mandatory in the Old Testament.

Offering or Free-Will Offering

How one should give to the Church:

- *Freely*

  Give and it shall be given unto you, good measure, pressed down, and shaken together, and running over, shall men give into your bosom. For with the same measure that you mete withal it shall be measured to you again. (Luke 6:38)

- *Regularly*

  Upon the first day of the week let every one of you lay by him in the store, as God hath prospered him. (1 Corinthians 16:2)

- *Cheerfully*

Every man according as he purposeth in his heart, so let him give, not grudging, or of necessity: for God loveth a cheerful giver. (2 Corinthians 9:7)

- *Not Grudgingly*

But a certain man named Ananias, with Sapphira his wife, sold a possession,
    And kept back part of the price, his wife also being privy to it, and brought a certain part, and laid it at the Apostles feet.
    But Peter said, "Ananias why hath Satan filled thine heart to lie to the Holy Ghost, and to keep back part of the price of the land?
    Whiles it remained, was it not thine own? And after it was sold was it not in thine own power? Why hast thou conceived this thing in thine heart? Thou hast not lied unto men, but unto God." (Acts 5:1–4)

The land was theirs, and the money they sold it for was theirs, but they made a pledge to give it all, only to withhold a portion of it.
    Your possession is in your hand to do whatever or to give whatever; that power is in your hand, but whatever you give, give it from the heart. We must be careful with the vows we make.
    The book of Ecclesiastes 5:4–5 teaches us, "When thou vowest a vow unto God, defer not to pay it, for he hath no pleasure in fools."

Better is it that thou shouldest not vow, than that shouldest vow and not pay. (Ecclesiastes 5:5)

You give because you are blessed, so give to be a blessing to someone.

Paul wrote to the church at Corinthians 16:1–3, "Now concerning the collection for the saints, as I have given order to the churches of Galatia, even so do."

> Upon the first day of the week let every one of
> you lay by him in store, as God hath prospered
> him, that there be no gathering when I come. (1
> Corinthians 16:2)

It appears here that there was some confusion about the offering collected at the church in Corinthians, and the distribution was not distributed as it should have. He referred them to take the pattern of them in Galatia and do the same as they do.

It's imperative for the churches to collect the free-will offering on the first day of the week or any day that a free-will offering is given.

In the church, we only have one high priest, in the person of our Lord and Savior, Jesus Christ, and He was called after the order of Melchizedek; and not after the order of Aaron (Hebrews 7:12):

> For the priesthood being changed, there is made
> of the necessity a change also of the law.

Give because you love:

> And though I bestow all my goods to the poor,
> and though I give my body to be burned, and
> have not Love or charity, it profiteth me nothing.
> (1 Corinthians 13:3)

Please don't be afraid to give to the church; whether a dime or a dollar, give it from your heart, and for the love of Christ and the church. Amen. To God be the glory.

About the Author

Conrad C. Henry Sr. was born on the island of Antigua, West Indies, in Bolands Village. He attended the Goodwill Academy School and is now living in the USA. He obtained his GED in New York City and was called into the ministry by God the Father through Jesus Christ His Lord and Savior. Conrad was ordained by the Goodwill Baptist Association in Bronx, New York.

His concern and inspiration for the articles he wrote, "Losing the Image of God and Tithes and Offering," was impressed upon his heart by the Holy Spirit. In fact, he reveals every word and event to create the understanding of each topic. Conrad's hope is that these articles will help someone to put their complete trust in God through *Jesus* Christ the Lord. May God be praised.

CPSIA information can be obtained
at www.ICGtesting.com
Printed in the USA
BVHW081702090123
655918BV00016B/199

9 781684 989652